THE PEOPLE WORK:
AMERICAN PERSPECTIVES,
1840–1940

Front cover:
Charles Frederick Ulrich,
The Village Printing Shop, Haarlem, Holland, 1884.
Frontispiece:
Winslow Homer, *Haymakers*, 1867.

Published in conjunction with the exhibitions organized
by Elizabeth Kennedy,
Terra Museum of American Art, Chicago
and Katherine M. Bourguignon,
Musée d'Art Américain Giverny, France:
The People Work: American Perspectives, 1840–1940,
Terra Museum of American Art, Chicago (March 15–May 25, 2003) and
Le Travail à l'œuvre : les artistes américains, 1840–1940,
Musée d'Art Américain Giverny, France (June 15–August 17, 2003).

Produced by the Department of Publications,
Musée d'Art Américain Giverny
Designed by Studio Le Petit Didier

ISBN: 0–932171–29–X

Published by the Musée d'Art Américain Giverny
99, rue Claude Monet, 27620 Giverny, France
(www.maag.org)

Printed and bound in Belgium

CONTENTS

05

Terra Foundation for the Arts was established in 1978 with a mission to acquire, preserve, exhibit, and interpret original works of art to foster a greater understanding and appreciation of America's rich artistic and cultural heritage. It oversees the operations of the Terra Museum of American Art and the Musée d'Art Américain Giverny, supporting their exhibitions, scholarly publications and educational agendas. The two museums share a collection that was begun by Daniel J. Terra. The current exhibition is fourth in a series of exhibitions entitled "American Perspectives" that demonstrates the depth and breadth of Terra's collecting vision. The first three exhibitions in the series—*The City and the Country* (1999), *Waves and Waterways* (2000) and *The Extraordinary and The Everyday* (2001)—which were organized by Derrick Cartwright, former director of the Musée d'Art Américain Giverny, initiated thematic approaches by which to consider the collection.

The People Work: American Perspectives, 1840–1940, organized by Elizabeth Kennedy, curator at Terra Museum of American Art, pursues a similar direction and considers why certain images of labor in American art have become emblems of national identity, while others portray laborers and the act of labor in a purely romanticized light. In her essay, Kennedy convincingly argues that the heroes of the American pastoral tradition—the Yankee farmer and his modern counterpart the Western cowboy—are linked iconic figures that celebrate both a political and economic philosophy. Katherine Bourguignon, assistant curator at the Musée d'Art Américain Giverny, provides an insightful introduction that explores the historical attitudes and philosophical points of view that have shaped America's ideas about the nature and definition of labor throughout the nineteenth and twentieth centuries. Through ideas and theories such as those associated with Karl Marx and Hannah Arendt, Bourguignon creates a framework in which Kennedy's ideas can be mapped.

The People Work considers the latent as well as the conventional meanings of images of labor in American art. By exploring diverse representations from the Terra Foundation for the Arts collection and several key works on loan, it encourages us to consider a variety of human activity as labor and to question common assumptions and attitudes on its unique history in the United States. The following essays and the accompanying exhibition are perfectly aligned with the Terra mission—to explore America's rich artistic and cultural heritage through its art. My sincerest appreciation is extended to our dedicated staffs for continuing to realize this important goal.

PREFACE

ELIZABETH GLASSMAN
DIRECTOR, TERRA MUSEUMS
EXECUTIVE VICE-PRESIDENT,
TERRA FOUNDATION FOR THE ARTS

This exhibition and its related publication have called upon the expertise of staffs from both Terra Foundation for the Arts museums. Colleagues provided encouragement and support in the many aspects that lead to a successful project. I extend my thanks at Terra Museum of American Art to Kristina Bottomley, Tim Duncan, Laura Kalas, Leo Kelly, Cathy Ricciardelli, and Tom Skwerski; and at Musée d'Art Américain Giverny to Didier Dauvel, Didier Guiot, Bronwyn Griffith, Sophie Lévy, Véronique Roca, and Olivier Touren for all their work in making this exhibition a success at both museums.

Critical comments on my essay by Katherine Bourguignon, Wendy Greenhouse, Jan McNeill, and Shelly Roman were invaluable. Francesca Rose's publication expertise and unfailing attention to detail has earned her a special debt of thanks. Sarah Blackwood deserves particular appreciation for her editorial craftsmanship, and Claire Guilloteau for her assistance in editing, proofreading, and obtaining artists' rights for the catalogue.

Key loans were critical to the realization of this exhibition and I am most appreciative to the following museums for lending their important paintings. My thanks to Director Rick Stewart and Chief Curator Jane Myers at the Amon Carter Museum in Fort Worth, Texas; Vice-President and Chief Curatorial Officer James Nottage at the Eiteljorg Museum of American Indians and Western Art in Indianapolis, Indiana; and Curator Sarah E. Boehme at the Whitney Gallery of Western Art at the Buffalo Bill Historical Center in Cody, Wyoming.

I owe a debt of gratitude to Elizabeth Glassman who challenged me to consider how two culturally diverse audiences would benefit from innovative approaches to interpreting American art. This exhibition, organized by the Terra Museum of American Art in Chicago and exhibited also at its sister museum, the Musée d'Art Américain Giverny, provides another important milestone in reassessing the transatlantic connections of American art. Thank you to the Terra Foundation for the Arts Board of Trustees for their continued commitment in supporting such scholarly endeavors.

ELIZABETH KENNEDY
CURATOR, TERRA MUSEUM
OF AMERICAN ART

07

GEORGE BENJAMIN LUKS
KNITTING FOR THE SOLDIERS:
HIGH BRIDGE PARK, C. 1918

08

KATHERINE
M. BOURGUIGNON, PH.D.
ASSISTANT CURATOR,
MUSÉE D'ART AMÉRICAIN GIVERNY

Chalfant's painting is nostalgic in its portrayal of this solitary worker in a highly detailed style at such a late date. By 1907, factories and mass production had already started to become the main force of the American economy, gradually replacing artisan production. With the growth of capitalism and wage labor, the self-reliant craftsman became obsolete, giving way to a worker alienated from the product of his labor. This old man continuing in dignity to produce objects independently by hand evokes feelings for a quickly disappearing past.

While *The Blacksmith* fits easily within preconceived notions of labor, showing a man physically at work, another painting from this time period expands this definition. In *Knitting for the Soldiers* (p. 8), George Luks painted a group of women seated outdoors in a snow-filled park. Each woman bends over her handiwork, knitting in quiet camaraderie. The skilled but unpaid effort of these women also represents an American attitude to work. Like the blacksmith, these women evidence dignity as they gather to produce utilitarian objects, this time for charity. The bright colors of Luks's more modernist painting contrast sharply with Chalfant's earth-toned naturalism, but both pictures define artisanship as worthwhile—work as central to one's existence.

The American paintings and prints gathered in this exhibition do not show a revolutionary attitude toward work. Instead of oppressed workers or strong political messages, the pictures

Two pictures from the early twentieth century mark the vast thematic territory of *The People Work: American Perspectives 1840–1940*. In *The Blacksmith* (fig. 1), Jefferson David Chalfant depicted an older, bearded man in his workshop, surrounded by the tools of his trade. With one hand he holds a metal rod against his anvil, its tip glowing red-hot. With the other hand he prepares to strike it with a hammer and physically shape it into a utilitarian object. Not glorified nor idealized, the worker nevertheless exudes a noble serenity and independence in his task. His white shirt glows clean in the rough environment of the workshop, and light falls on his balding head drawing attention perhaps to his clear mind. In nineteenth-century America people believed that a worker owned his own labor and could reap the success of his effort.

INTRODUCTION

1. JEFFERSON DAVID CHALFANT

THE BLACKSMITH, 1907

emphasize the nobility of the worker and his or her direct link to the tools of a trade. There are exceptions that highlight exploitative working conditions (such as *Sweat Shop* by Boris Gorelick [fig. 2] or *Striptease at New Gotham* by Reginald Marsh [fig. 3]) and there are images that can be read in multiple ways—as representations of both work and leisure (such as Shinn, *Theater Scene* [p. 43] or Marsh, *Pip and Flip* [p. 48]). For the most part, however, American artists active between 1840 and 1940 avoided scenes of over-crowded factories as well as depictions of slavery, preferring to appeal to their audience with images of noble, hard-working people that could help define a growing national identity.

From Skilled Craftsman to Wage Laborer

Writing in England, Karl Marx (1818–83) developed radical ideas about the alienation of the worker from the product of his labor and explained the limitations of capitalism. As he wrote in 1844, "The worker is related to the product of his labor as to an alien object.... The worker puts his life into the object; and now it no longer belongs to him, it belongs to the object.... The more the worker produces, the less he has to consume; the more values he creates, the less value, the less dignity, he has...."[1] Americans found much to admire in Marx's belief that labor was the fundamental factor in modern society and that man's essential identity was that of worker. After all, Americans had long extolled the moral and social qualities of work as well as the possibility, through work, for self-expression and development. And as America moved into the period of industrial capitalism, the Marxist discourse of the alienated

worker and the need for reform became even more valuable. But while Marxist ideas led to revolt in France, a labor party in England, and full-fledged communism in Russia, Americans were often hesitant to embrace the revolutionary quality of his message.[2] Instead, they worked for social reform and better working conditions all the while building their capitalist economy.

From 1840 to 1940, the United States witnessed a gradual transition from an economy propelled by the independent farmer and skilled worker to the development of industrial capitalism and wage-labor. By 1850, the majority of the population in the United States still lived in rural areas and worked in agriculture, only about 14% worked in manufacturing, but these numbers would change radically over the next fifty to seventy years.[3] The transition to a reliance on factories and a capitalist economy immediately following the Civil War allowed for social change and created ambiguous roles for the worker. Political activists spoke of the advantages and disadvantages of mass-produced labor, extolling American factories as the lifeblood of the country while striving for labor reform. French artists shared this conflicted response to the industrial revolution, producing during this period both glorifications of industry and rural labor as well as scenes of alienated workers and oppressed peasants. For example, whereas Rosa Bonheur

1. Karl Marx, "Alienated Labour" 1844 as cited and contextualized in Melissa Dabakis, *Visualizing Labor in American Sculpture: Monuments, Manliness, and the Work Ethic, 1880–1935* (Cambridge: Cambridge University Press, 1999): 14. For a longer selection from this essay and more information about Karl Marx, see especially *The Portable Karl Marx*, ed. Eugene Kamenka (New York: Penguin Books, 1983).
2. For discussions of the American influence of Karl Marx, see Ian Tyrell, *The Absent Marx: Class Analysis and Liberal History in Twentieth-Century America* (Westport, Conn.: Greenwood Press, 1986) and Earl Browder, *Marx and America: A Study of the Doctrine of Impoverishment* (Westport, Conn.: Greenwood Press, 1974).
3. Sean Wilentz, "Society, Politics, and the Market Revolution, 1815–1848," in *The New American History*, ed. Eric Foner (Philadelphia: Temple University, 1990): 51–71.

3. REGINALD MARSH

STRIPTEASE AT NEW GOTHAM, 1935

2. BORIS GORELICK

SWEAT SHOP, C. 1936–39

4. Hannah Arendt, *Condition de l'homme moderne*, traduit de l'anglais par Georges Fradier (Paris: Calmann-Lévy, 1961 and 1983).

painted competent field hands in works such as *Plowing in the Nivernais: The Dressing of Vines*, 1849 (Paris, Musée d'Orsay), Gustave Courbet emphasized the exhaustion of physical labor in *The Stonebreakers* of the same year (now destroyed).

The American paintings and prints in this exhibition do not all easily fit this steady progression from skilled craftsman to wage-laborer. As many of the pictures demonstrate, artists preferred to represent nostalgic scenes of independent workers and farmers in harmony with the land instead of overworked factory employees or businessmen. Another reason why the images fail to map a clear development of the economic trend in the United States is the broad understanding of work that they provide. A woman sewing in her home (p. 47), a model posing nude for an artist (p. 49), a shop-owner on a Parisian street corner (fig. 4)—such pictures extend our understanding of what work means, calling up not only Marxism but also distinctions made by German-born philosopher Hannah Arendt (1906–75) among labor, work, and action. In *The Human Condition*, 1958, Arendt linked "labor" with animal activity destined for survival and "work" with human intervention that led to something more permanent.[4] Searching for food would be labor while building a house would be work. Labor is unending and impermanent while work transforms nature according to human needs, leading to permanence and becoming a public concern. Arendt's final category of human activity, "action," is linked with plurality and freedom, involving the human possibility to create something new, to act and interact with each other. In many of these images, artists emphasized a group element as well as the possibility for transcendence through individual work or the chance to reach others through physical and intellectual effort. This notion of interactivity among humans relates to Arendt's ultimate argument, that humans are social beings, expressing freedom only in their interaction with one another. In the essay that follows and the exhibition that accompanies it, we should consider all human activity (paid or unpaid, skilled or unskilled) as related to the notion of work.

Paintings of Peasants in Europe and America

One category of images in this exhibition will be familiar to European and American audiences and deserves further contextualization. Images of rural labor dominated the late nineteenth century in America as collectors began to seek out depictions of peasants by French artists like Jean-François Millet or Jules Breton. These nostalgic representations of peaceful harmony with nature, paired with a naturalistic style, appealed to many Americans concerned with the changing roles of rural and

4. FRANK MYERS BOGGS

STREET SCENE IN PARIS, 1878

urban workers as industrial capitalism gained ground. Eager to translate a foreign symbol into one of their own, wealthy Americans purchased paintings of French peasants for private and public collections.

French critics saw representations of peasants both positively (as sober, pious figures faithful to the past) and negatively (as primitive, uneducated people who posed a threat of class struggle). This contradictory interpretation of a common symbol became focused, by 1865, on the works of Millet and Breton. Critics argued that Millet painted a misanthropic and untamed nature, highlighting the poverty-stricken peasant, while Breton emphasized the dignity of work and the potential for harmony with nature.[5] Breton's works (p. 20), they suggested, told stories about simple people living in and of the earth. Millet's paintings, on the other hand, contained a hidden and dangerous potential of workers unsatisfied with a difficult life and ready to revolt. This opposition between "noble peasants" and "exploited workers" pervaded French art criticism of the time and found its way into American journalism as well, as Laura Meixner has demonstrated. In 1899, for example, a journalist in the San Francisco Examiner wrote a poem about one of Millet's well-known paintings *Man with a Hoe* (fig. 5) in which he called for social reform for American farmers. This poem led many middleclass Americans to consider the image as a reference to a wide range of rural problems.[6] In 1912 another famous painting by Millet, *The Gleaners*, 1857 (Paris, Musée d'Orsay), appeared in an American newspaper in the form of a satirical cartoon about capitalist exploitation of labor while just a few years earlier the same painting had appeared on the cover of a seed catalogue as the promise of plentiful rural harvests.[7] Such diverse use of the same image underscores its multiple readings. *The Gleaners* could be used to symbolize oppressed workers and harmonious farming. Such divergent interpretations demonstrate that

Americans felt the ambiguous messages of these paintings of peasants, and that they altered their meanings by appropriating and decontextualizing them. As Laura Meixner has noted, "When Americans 'translated' French images, they took possession by interpreting."[8]

The Gleaners and other paintings of peasants by Millet and members of the Barbizon school had already become associated in the American mentality with the institution of slavery, and many critics would expand on the similarity of the European peasant and the American slave. At the same time, however, Americans often voiced a sense of superiority over their European counterparts, celebrating the Yankee farmer and degrading the European peasant. As one Ohio farmer said in the late nineteenth century, "In Europe labor is accustomed to oppression, and it's a hard part of God's destiny for them, to be borne patiently... [but] our people have been carefully educated to consider themselves the best on earth, and they will not patiently submit

5. Neil McWilliam, "Le Paysan au Salon: Critique d'art et construction d'une classe sous le Second empire," in *La Critique d'art en France 1850–1900* (Saint-Étienne: CIEREC and Université de Saint-Étienne, 1989): 81-85.

6. Dabakis, p. 20. "To many, the phrase "man with a hoe" assumed a much broader meaning, serving as a code for rural degradation and industrial unrest."

7. These examples and much of my thinking about the interpretation of Millet's paintings in America come from Laura Meixner, *French Realist Painting and the Critique of American Society, 1865–1900* (Cambridge: Cambridge University Press, 1995): 12. See also Peter Bermingham, "Artful and playful Peasants," in *American Art in the Barbizon Mood* (Washington, D.C.: Smithsonian Institution Press, 1975) and Lois Marie Fink, "French Art in the United States, 1850–70," *Gazette des Beaux-Arts* (September 1978): 87-100.

8. Meixner, p. 4.

5. JEAN-FRANÇOIS MILLET (1814—75)

MAN WITH A HOE, 1860—62

OIL ON CANVAS, 31 1/2 X 39 IN. (80 X 99 CM)

THE J. PAUL GETTY MUSEUM,

LOS ANGELES, 85.PA.114

12

9. Cited in Leon Fink, "American Labor History," in *The New American History*, ed. Eric Foner (Philadelphia: Temple University, 1990): 241.

10. Homer saw Millet's *The Gleaners* in 1867 at the Exposition Universelle in Paris and found inspiration in many works by Barbizon artists. See Kenneth Haltman, "Antipastoralism in Early Winslow Homer," *Art Bulletin* (March 1998): 100.

to privation such as this system is leading to."9 Such blatant expression of superiority over European peasants explains yet another attraction of these pictures for an American audience who often viewed them as charming representations of the Old World.

American artists tended to avoid strong political statement when they painted scenes of peasants and instead emphasized men and women in harmony with nature. Their paintings of the 1860s and 1870s echoed the transcendental writings of Ralph Waldo Emerson (1803–82) and Henry David Thoreau (1817–62), so popular in America at the time. These two American authors found moral, spiritual values in natural phenomena and encouraged people to live in community with nature. Winslow Homer found great inspiration in French paintings of peasants and rural workers during his yearlong visit to France in 1866–67.10 In two of the pictures he painted during that trip, *Haymakers* (fig. 6) and *Gleaners* (p. 33), Homer represented men and women in the fields, bent over their difficult physical labor or carrying large instruments of their work, but not oppressed. Instead, the harmonious compositions and rhythmic use of color convince us of the fair treatment these

people have received and of their acceptance of the life they lead. Childe Hassam and Louis Paul Dessar depicted individual women in the fields turned away from the viewer. These two paintings share an interest in visually connecting the woman with the land. In his painting (p. 14), Dessar extended the pink of the woman's dress into the fields around her and placed a high horizon above her head to visually imbed her into the land. In his picture (p. 40), Hassam painted a younger girl who looks thoughtfully out at the fields, her head just above the horizon line, dressed in colors that echo the land around her. Like Homer, both Hassam and Dessar emphasize a peaceful communion with nature.

These nostalgic images from the late nineteenth century share themes with other works of this time period as the emphasis shifted in America from free craftsman to wage laborer. By showing innocent farmers and peasants, not downtrodden but in harmony with nature, American artists could shift attention away from growing industrial worries. In the essay that follows, Elizabeth Kennedy places these rural images into a broader context as she explores the historical and artistic attitudes to work in American society throughout this time period. Perhaps the message to be drawn from this particular selection of images from the Terra Foundation for the Arts collection is not that of downtrodden laborer, but rather of the necessity for useful activity and the fundamental role of work in the modern American society.

13

6. WINSLOW HOMER

HAYMAKERS, 1867

14

LOUIS PAUL DESSAR

PEASANT WOMAN AND HAYSTACKS,

GIVERNY, 1892

1. Thomas Jefferson, *Notes on the State of Virginia*, ed. William Peden (Chapel Hill: University of North Carolina Press, 1955) query XIX quoted in Harold Spencer, "J. Alden Weir and the Image of the American Farm," in *A Connecticut Place: Weir Farm An American Painter's Rural Retreat* (Wilton, Conn.: Weir Farm Trust and The National Park Service, 2000): 46.

2. Quoted in Brice Bustard, *A New Deal for the Arts* (Seattle: University of Washington Press, 1997): 49.

3. I am indebted to Harold Spencer's concise overview of the literary tradition of the American pastoral in "J. Alden Weir and the Image of the American Farm," in *A Connecticut Place: Weir Farm An American Painter's Rural Retreat* (Wilton, Conn.: Weir Farm Trust and The National Park Service, 2000): 42–75.

4. Genesis 4: 1–3.

"[T]hose who labor in the earth are the chosen people of God, if ever he had a chosen people, whose breasts he has made his peculiar deposit for substantial and genuine virtue." [1]
Thomas Jefferson (1743–1826),
Notes on the State of Virginia, 1785

"Always the heart and soul of our country will be the heart and soul of the common man." [2]
Franklin Delano Roosevelt (1882–1945),
November 2, 1940

Inspired by the ideals of democracy, political leaders from Thomas Jefferson to Franklin Delano Roosevelt evoked the quintessential American citizen as one who works. From its inception as a nation, America valued the economic doctrines of individualism and entrepreneurialism embodied most frequently in depictions of workers associated with the unspoiled landscape of the New World—the Yankee farmer and later the Western cowboy. In the eighteenth century, the Jeffersonian yeoman, a small landholder, transformed a wilderness into a republic and linked the potential for equal opportunity to an Arcadian utopia. A century later, the emerging dominance of industrial capitalism created a new vision of the American worker that, paradoxically, retained an allegiance to the notion of a pastoral setting —the unfettered cowboy in the wilderness.

THE ICONIC AND THE INVISIBLE

ELIZABETH KENNEDY
CURATOR, TERRA MUSEUM
OF AMERICAN ART,
CHICAGO

The "knight of the plains," a distinctive American contribution to popular culture, became an emblem of personal liberty in an era characterized by the unbridled laissez-faire capitalism of the so-called "robber barons." Rarely, despite changing historical circumstances in the twentieth century, did images of the predominately urban American workforce replace these pastoral icons of labor as representative of national identity. Imbued with the ideology of the Puritan work ethic, American artists did at times create images of labor in a variety of subjects and artistic styles but, significantly, not as a glorification of national values. Scenes of unmistakable labor are hardly ever represented overtly. The subtext of many paintings, however, can be read as examples of an individual's labor or industriousness, veiled by another's leisure or transformed by the artist's nostalgic point of view into a picturesque fantasy. Whether unequivocally portrayed as symbols of national identity or ambiguously acknowledged, compelling images of labor in this exhibition, drawn primarily from the Terra Foundation for the Arts collection, narrate an American perspective on people at work.

The American Pastoral Tradition

The necessity of developing a new national identity after the American Revolution (1773–83) encouraged a discourse on defining what it meant to be an American. Political philosophers turned to texts from antiquity and biblical scripture for inspiration.[3] From Virgil's *Georgics* and *Eclogues*, paeans to alternative visions of the Arcadian pastoral landscape, America's founding fathers chose the patrician farmer—representing land ownership not fieldwork—to represent the promise of their democratic experiment. The agricultural arts of tilling and planting were favored over shepherds soothing their flocks with music. Interestingly, biblical iconography also shares this dichotomy between pastoral ideals of the farmer and the shepherd. The sons of Adam and Eve represent the archetypal agricultural workers: Cain a farmer and Abel a shepherd.[4] America's Protestant citizenry chose the "hard work" of the farmer as the preferred pastoral model to create a "fruitful land" out of a wilderness.

The Citizen-Farmer:
A National Icon

The cult of the farmer as a national symbol was enhanced by America's famous Protestant work ethic. English colonists brought the tenets of Puritanism based on Calvinism to the New World: self-reliance, frugality and unremitting labor. They believed hard work to be a religious duty that brought salvation and material rewards. In an agrarian colonial economy, their proto-capitalist beliefs, however, encouraged trade and production. In 1782, Hector St. John de Crèvecœur described his fellow Americans as "a people of cultivators... we are animated with the spirit of an industry that is unfettered and unrestrained, because each person works for himself...."[5]

The association of work, the American landscape, and citizenship began with the colonial farmer, who as a landowner was eligible to vote. In post-revolutionary America, the republican exemplum—the farmer as citizen-soldier—was formalized by the founding in 1783 of the Society of Cincinnatus in emulation of the fifth century B.C. patrician who reluctantly left his farm to lead the Roman armies against their enemies. The landscape in *View of a Manor House on the Harlem River, New York* (p. 31) transforms a pastoral scene composed of classical landscape conventions into one that represents a democratic landscape with the farm laborer in the middle-ground as a cipher for the family who owned the Manhattan Island estate.

In most states by the 1830s, property ownership was no longer necessary for white male enfranchisement—the nation's only voting population. During the escalating sectional strife in the late 1840s over slavery in the Southern states and its potential expansion into Western territories, the positive political aura that surrounded the farmer faded. It would regain momentum with the Homestead Act of 1862, an important if ultimately unsuccessful, campaign to grant land in the Western territories to individuals who improved the property through their labor. Yet after the Civil War, the pictorial revival of the farmer as citizen-hero, the embodiment of a national democratic lesson, lost its potency once again.

Portrayals of farmers at work in the field are rare; typically they are represented in genre paintings that emphasize characteristics associated with the quick-witted yeoman.[6] Yet these genre paintings of rural inhabitants are more than anecdotes of rural mannerisms, they congratulate the success of a free market economic system where Yankee ideals of frugality, industry, and a healthy skepticism are rewarded with tempting material goods as depicted in *The Yankee Pedlar* (fig. 1). The paintings also serve as sermons on the virtues of rural enterprise, exemplified by *The Trap Sprung* (fig. 2), where Yankee ingenuity not brute strength rules the day, teaching that resourcefulness overcomes the necessity of exhausting manual labor.

The late-nineteenth-century success of American agribusiness increasingly separated the contemporary farmer from the artist's picturesque motif. A mechanical reaper for harvesting, invented by Chicago's Cyrus H. McCormick (1809–94), was patented in 1834 and available internationally

5. Hector St. John de Crèvecœur, *Letters from an American Farmer and Sketches of Eighteenth Century America* (New York: Penguin Classics, 1988): 69. For the most comprehensive review of American pastoral paintings see Sarah Burns, *Pastoral Inventions: Rural Life in Nineteenth-Century American Art and Culture* (Philadelphia: Temple University Press, 1989).

6. The importance of the Yankee farmer in American art is discussed in Elizabeth Johns, "An Image of Pure Yankeeism," in *American Genre Painting: the Politics of Everyday Life* (New Haven: Yale University Press, 1991): 24–59.

2. WILLIAM SIDNEY MOUNT

THE TRAP SPRUNG, 1844

16

1. THOMAS WATERMAN WOOD

THE YANKEE PEDLAR, 1872

7. Samuel Isham, *History of American Painting* (1905), rev. ed. with Royal Cortissoz (New York: Macmillan, 1927): 495, quoted in Burns, *Pastoral Inventions*, p. 225.

8. Elizabeth Johns, "Settlement and Development: Claiming the West," in *The West as America: Reinterpreting Images of the Frontier* (Washington, D.C.: National Museum of American Art, 1991): 191–236.

by 1851. With the exception of commercial brochures and the occasional Currier and Ives prints, however, imagery of farming technology was unusual. After the turn of the century, art critic Samuel Isham summed up Americans' view of the modern farmer over the past few decades: "[farmers are] too independent, too sophisticated; his machinery, his reapers and threshers lacked the epic note; they were new like his clothes, his house, all his surroundings."[7]

Art patrons who shared Isham's assessment favored images that romanticized primitive agriculture practice, especially harvesting by hand. American artists reinforced the morals inherent to traditional rural iconography—honoring the rewards of individual enterprise, reaping the abundance of advance planning and hard work— for an urban audience. Harvesting, as a metaphor, extends into various industries related to gathering nature's bounty. The harvesting of forests for personal use, as in the clearing of land for farming in *Hunter Mountain, Twilight* (fig. 3), was a powerful symbol for the self-reliance of the individual— a model for the entrepreneurial capitalist.

"Harvesting the sea," as with agricultural subjects in the nineteenth century, was associated with biblical imagery. The labors of fishermen, for example in *Gloucester Harbor* (p. 34), could serve as a symbol for the industriousness of the wider community. By the century's end, nostalgic views of an old-fashioned American farm or a quaint seaside village often lost their moral message and served more as a promotion for tourism and an escape from urban industrialism's unpleasantness. Generations later, during the troubled economic times of the 1930s, American artists sought out the "primitive" conditions of America's fishing villages to expand their repertoire of images of the worker. The extreme physical efforts of fishermen were idealized as heroic acts and, once again, were emblems of the strength of their community as depicted by *The Swordfisherman* (p. 50).

The meaning of country life in America changed as the nation evolved into a modern industrial society throughout the early nineteenth century. Conventional political ideals during President Andrew Jackson's administration (1829–37) continued to promote the farmer as a symbol of democratic values and American individualism. Respect for the rural population, however, diminished as urban populations grew larger and national boundaries pushed further West. Negative stereotypes of rural folk were savored by the smug middle-class citizenry of Eastern cities as picturesque moments of a bygone past.[8] An underlying condescending attitude towards provincial folk's labor found expression in portrayals such as *The Jolly Flatboatmen* (fig. 4), a depiction of the legendary wild men of the river, whose spirited amusements masked the brute strength needed to maneuver the clumsy vehicle. Nevertheless, America's belief in hard work as the driving force for success was unfaltering.

At the height of the Gilded Age in late-nineteenth-century America, the escalating tensions between free-market entrepreneurs and a largely immigrant, urban labor force lessened

17

3. SANFORD ROBINSON GIFFORD

HUNTER MOUNTAIN, TWILIGHT, 1866

4. GEORGE CALEB BINGHAM

THE JOLLY FLATBOATMEN, 1877–78

the philosophical value of the farmer as a cultural symbol for an egalitarian social order. The mythologizing of rural values did not diminish, however, as new protagonists—French peasants and the American cowboy—simultaneously began to appear in American art, displacing the farmer as the dominant symbol of the rural American worker. On one hand, the paintings of pious European peasants, usually women standing in cultivated fields content with their humble rank in the hierarchy of workers, were reassuring to elites who dealt with dissatisfied laborers, often male immigrants, in the workplace (p. 14). Conversely, images of the physically robust cowboy on horseback appealed to frustrated industrial managers as a worker who controlled his own destiny (fig. 5).

What is immediately striking is the gendered divergence of these representations of the rural laborer and their respective appeal to different audiences. Genteel society's penchant for paintings of an orderly cultivated landscape adorned with demure, beautiful young women was less about nostalgia for an bygone era than a soothing visual tonic in a contemporary world beset by class conflict. The popularity of French peasant imagery in the homes of the elites of New York and Boston, the epicenters of European immigration, reassured art patrons of their social superiority over the nation's newest citizenry.[9] Similar anxieties arising in the workplace about labor-capital relationships prompted male, corporate managers to find solace in depictions of cowboys enjoying unmitigated freedom in the hyper-masculine territory of the Western wilderness. Surprisingly, these two diametrically opposed views of the worker in a pastoral landscape, one a European female toiler in a domesticated field and the other an American male free spirit in the wilderness, remained potent until the 1940s.[10]

The European Peasant: A Romantic Appropriation

The vogue for paintings of peasants became an international phenomenon as tensions between labor and capital increased in an expanding industrial age.[11] The American art lover's fascination with the French peasant, beginning in the 1850s with the Barbizon landscape school, is exceptional in its appropriation of another nation's patriotic symbol. For the East Coast elite, the farmer's appeal as an exemplar of American rural values was displaced onto European peasant imagery that to the eyes of a foreigner retained its innocence and virtue as the ideal community.

In the two decades following the Civil War, Americans traveled in increasingly large numbers to France. The substantial number of artists that enrolled in French art academies were inspired not only by the excellence of instruction but also the growing demand by wealthy American patrons for the imprimatur of French artistic training. One of the most fascinating aspects of this interaction between American artist and patron was a demand for anecdotal tableaux or observations of daily life of French peasants—the most popular of all subjects submitted by American artists to the Paris Salons.[12]

Study in America of prints that replicated the Barbizon masters' paintings of peasants was as influential to American artists as their summers spent working at artists' colonies in the French countryside.[13] Of remarkable interest was their

9. For an insightful discussion of the cultural implications of evolutionary notions applied to class distinctions see Kathleen A. Pyne, *Art and the Higher Life: Painting and Evolutionary Thought in Late-Nineteenth-Century America* (Austin: University of Texas Press, 1996).

10. For the persistence of a reverence for a utopian past see T. J. Jackson Lears, *No Place of Grace: Antimodernism and the Transformation of American Culture, 1880–1920* (Chicago: The University of Chicago Press, 1981).

11. See particularly Peter Bermingham, *American Art in the Barbizon Mood* (Washington, D.C.: Smithsonian Institution Press, 1975), Richard R. Brettell and Caroline B. Brettell, *Painters and Peasants in the Nineteenth-Century* (New York: Rizzoli, 1983), and Robert Herbert's "City vs. Country: The Rural Images in French Paintings from Millet to Gauguin," *Artforum* 8 (February 1970): 44–55.

12. Lois Marie Fink, *American Art at the Nineteenth-Century Paris Salon* (Cambridge: Cambridge University Press, 1990): 72–74, 204.

13. A contextual overview of French artists' colonies is discussed in Nina Lübbren, "Painted Peasants," in *Rural Artists' Colonies in Europe 1870–1910* (New Brunswick, N.J.: Rutgers University Press, 2001). See Robert Herbert, *Peasants and "Primitivism": French Prints from Millet to Gauguin* (South Hadley: Mount Holyoke College Art Museum, 1995) for artists' study of prints.

5. FREDERIC REMINGTON

TRAILING TEXAS CATTLE, C. 1904

14. Burns, Brettell and among others discuss the contrast between the idealization of the French peasant women to Americans' aversion to women's manual labor in the fields.

15. From *The Crayon* 7 (October 1860) quoted in Lois Marie Fink *American Art at the Nineteenth-Century Paris Salon*, p. 72.

16. Henry David Thoreau's *Walden* (Boston: Houghton, Mifflin, 1882): 7, 10 quoted in Spencer *A Connecticut Place: Weir Farm An American Painter's Rural Retreat*, p. 47.

17. See Michael Jacobs, *The Good and Simple Life: Artists Colonies in Europe and America* (Oxford: Phaidon, 1985) for the similarities in French and American artists' colonies.

18. See Marshall W. Fishwick, "The Cowboy: America's Contribution to the World's Mythology," *Western Folklore* 11 (1951–52): 77–92, William H. Goetzmann and William N. Goetzmann, *The West of the Imagination* (New York: W. W. Norton Company, 1986), and Richard Slotkin, *Gunfighter Nation: The Myth of the Frontier in Twentieth-Century America* (New York: Harper Perennial, 1993).

interpretation of the rural French women working in the fields. Painted during his year in France in 1867, Winslow Homer's *The Gleaners* (p. 33) portrays a scene of rural charity, poor women were allowed to collect leftover grain after the official harvest was completed. Ironically, in principle if not always reality, American women, who actually worked in fields, were perceived, at times, as degraded by their fellow countrymen. Contemptuous comparisons were made about these rural women comparing them to European peasants or America's own black fieldhands.[14]

As financial disparity increased dramatically, patrons welcomed art where "[t]he people are kept down to picturesqueness, and are not allowed to get new fangled notions into their heads" safely containing the problematic concept of labor and self-reliance.[15] Occasionally, more realistic European agricultural workers, not romantic peasants, as seen in *Late Afternoon Sun* (p. 41), were portrayed reflecting Henry David Thoreau's unidealized view of the experience of pre-industrialized American farmers, whose "lives of quiet desperation" were burdened by "acres of land, tillage, mowing, pasture, and wood-lot."[16] Despite the popularity of European peasant paintings, American art critics complained of their artificiality and the lack of native subjects that were related to the American rural landscape or experience.

6. CHARLES M. RUSSELL

BRONC IN COW CAMP, 1897

The Cowboy: A New Pastoral Hero

Some French-trained American artists, who had previously portrayed European rural folks' quaint dress or archaic rituals, identified the same picturesque possibilities of their country's Southwestern "primitive" indigenous peoples while providing a recognizably American subject. By the 1880s, a few artists summered in New Mexico villages in emulation of their experiences in rural France.[17] They were captivated by the Native Americans' spiritual attachment to their pueblos and agricultural life as well as by their colorful costumes and ceremonies. Pueblo men, farmers as well as artisans then as now, were shown to be spiritually connected to the land through their direct contact with the soil. In *Making Pottery* (p. 45), the potter's hands shape the clay into a useful container and serves as a personification of many Anglo-Americans' fantasy about the Indians' individual autonomy and moral authenticity.

Other artists sought a new type of pastoral subject, definitively American but one that was celebratory of frontier settlement and the Western experience of Anglo-Americans.[18] The popularity of the cowboy, introduced as a new subject in "dime novels" in the 1860s, gained a popular audience. From 1883 to 1916, the fabled horseman was introduced as the showpiece of Buffalo Bill Cody's (1846–1917) incredibly successful Wild West Show, which toured the United States, England, and Europe. With the increasing popularity of "moving pictures" in the 1910s, the mythical cowboy was firmly established as the new American pastoral hero. Yet the working days of the cowboy as a professional cattle driver encompassed only a few decades, from the 1860s to 1890s. The humorous anecdotal details of range life that cowboy artist Charles M. Russell's *Bronc in Cow Camp* portrays satisfied the longing of an urban worker who imagined a life lived in the rugged outdoors (fig. 6).

19

Two Harvard University graduates share the responsibility for elevating the cowboy from Wild West entertainer to national emblem. Known as "that damned cowboy" by his political enemies, Theodore Roosevelt (1858–1919), who formed the Rough Riders to fight in the Spanish American War of 1898, lauded the cowboy for possessing "to a very high degree, the stern manly qualities that are invaluable to a nation."[19] During Roosevelt's presidency (1901–08), his friend Owen Wister's (1860–1938) novel, *The Virginian*, 1902, about a Wyoming cowboy whose primitive life provided the basis for an admirable moral code, made publishing history as edition after edition sold out. Significantly, the cowboy was more than an idolized historic figure; he was a return to America's earlier pastoral archetype of a citizen whose attachment to the land represented the democratic ideal of independent labor.

Throughout the first three decades of the twentieth century there was a small but steady demand from an Eastern clientele for paintings that depicted cowboys and the settling of the American West. In the 1940s when New York's modern art coterie reasserted its dominance over American Scene painters and regionalists in the American art world, all representations of laborers were critiqued as provincial and passé. New oil-rich patrons from Texas, Oklahoma, and California, however, sustained the popularity of the Western horseman in art. During World War II, the image of the cowboy emerged internationally as an icon of American individualism. The significance at the time of this anachronistic image of a man on horseback lies in his mastery over a wilderness—not a cultivated—landscape.

The persistence of an international audience for the cowboy, the male protagonist of as a genre in literature and film commonly characterized as "the Western," as a universal symbol representing freedom of action based on individual effort is unparalleled. Since the 1930s when the first museum of Western art, a collection comprised solely of depictions of "cowboys and Indians," opened in Montana, the cowboy as a national icon remains the most universally accepted emblem of the American worker or "common man" despite—or because of—its outsider status in the traditional art world.[20]

Within professional art circles, a popular audience's fascination with cowboys or European peasants in paintings was indicative of the art's unworthiness in the acceptable canon of modern art. French peasant paintings purchased by American elite and donated to art museums appealed to their middlebrow visitors. In a 1924 newspaper popularity poll, Jules Breton's *The Song of the Lark* (fig. 7) on exhibit at The Art Institute of Chicago was voted America's most popular painting much to the dismay of the museum's director who opted to take it off view, consigning it to museum storage.

Idealizing Images of Labor

The supremacy in American culture of the (white male) rural, independent worker—the political ideal of the voting citizen in America's democracy—carried such an ideological importance in the fine arts that other representations of labor were usually omitted. African American slaves, the unpaid workers of America's "peculiar institution," and Asian immigrants, who worked on the transcontinental railroad system and California's bonanza farms, are all but undetectable in the fine arts. Native Americans were stereotyped as savage warriors or decorative additions to a landscape. Women, half of the nation's work force, are rarely shown in occupations other than domestic tasks or those suited to their "feminine

19. From Theodore Roosevelt's *Ranch Life and the Hunting Trail* (1888) quoted in William W. Savage, Jr., *The Cowboy Hero: His Image in American History and Culture* (Norman, Oklahoma: University of Oklahoma Press, 1979): 98.

20. Elizabeth Kennedy, "Charlie Russell's Log Studio: The Origin of the Museum of Western Art," *Journal of the West* 40, no. 4 (Fall 2001): 60–66

20

7. JULES BRETON (1827–1906)

THE SONG OF THE LARK, 1884

OIL ON CANVAS, 43 1/2 X 33 1/4 IN. (110.6 X 85.8 CM)

THE ART INSTITUTE OF CHICAGO,

HENRY FIELD MEMORIAL COLLECTION, 1894.1033

21. Steven Adams, "Rural Images and the 1848 Revolution," in *The Barbizon School and the Origins of Impressionism* (London: Phaidon Press, 1994).

22. See Matthew Baigell, "American Art and National Identity: the 1920s," in *Critical Issues in American Art: A Book of Readings*, ed. Mary Ann Calo (Boulder: Westview Press, 1998): 269–84, Brice Bustard, *A New Deal for the Arts* (Seattle: University of Washington Press, 1997), and Melissa Dabakis, "The Individual vs. the Collective: Images of the American Worker in the 1920s," *The Journal of the Society for Industrial Archeology* 12, no. 2 (1986): 51–62.

23. Leo Marx, *The Machine in the Garden: Technology and the Pastoral Ideal in America* (London: Oxford University Press, 1964).

nature." In American works of art from this period, the almost total invisibility of strenuous labor by women, unless noticeably portrayed as European, and people of color serves to underline their marginal status as property owners or participants in a representative democracy. So-called unskilled laborers comprised principally of children, women, blacks, and recent immigrants, who had neither union nor political representation, were deemed unsuitable as symbols of national power or strength. Workers of marginal status were selected as pictorial subjects only when they were shown at leisure activities or as background foils to their societal betters.

Men's Skillful Work

Similarly absent from much of American art are images of men as industrial laborers either as a celebration of the free market system or a protest against intolerable working conditions. The overarching ideology of personal freedom and equality were so compelling—sparking revolutions in America in 1776, France in 1789, and in other European countries in the 1840s— and, apparently, so compromised in reality that artists rarely chose to disrupt the status quo of the upper-class art world with troubling scenes of conflict. As the rhetoric of nationalism began to dominate the international political scene in the 1910s, heroic images of male industrial workers began to appear in the fine arts,

reaching peak popularity in the 1930s, ironically, when unemployment was at its height. Thus in American art, the physically fit urban laborer briefly shared the honors with his equally vigorous rural counterpart.

The aestheticization of labor politics, associated with the European revolutions of 1848, defined the visual role of the working man and his importance in myth-making.[21] The growth of socialist political parties in Europe and the politicization of many European artists merged in a desire to create potent imagery that included the industrial worker and commemorated his productivity. In contrast, few American artists adopted socialism and a study of their art finds almost no imagery of the industrial worker until the 1920s when the United States emerged as an international industrial power.[22] The strife that existed between the working class and titans of American industry is, with few exceptions, never portrayed in art.

The denial of class differences in America was linked to the belief in "hard work" as the driving force in success. Just as images of the European rural worker were appropriated to present a non-threatening representation of labor, late nineteenth-century American artists' interpretation of the urban French worker paralleled the tendency to ennoble the individual or reduce him or her to a picturesque motif. Certain attributes of Parisian workers that were suitably "French" to the eye of an American—the inclusion of a laborer and his young daughter in *Une Averse, rue Bonaparte* (fig. 8)—also carried a potential ideological message in paintings that hinted at class differences that were disavowed in America.

Even during the early decades of the twentieth century when artists were portraying American men at work, a nostalgic lens remained the preeminent artistic strategy.[23] Pre-industrial workers in an agricultural setting found an urban equivalent in the portrayal of the specialized interiors of old-fashioned craftsmen. Patrons

8. FREDERICK CHILDE HASSAM

UNE AVERSE, RUE BONAPARTE, 1887

were reassured by images that celebrated venerated, if obsolete, skills. The labor-intensive preparations of these craftsmen in contrast to the repetitive motions of the factory worker celebrate a humane version of technology. *The Village Printing Shop, Haarlem, Holland* (p. 39) represents the labor-intensive preparations for printing by contrasting the apprentice's break to the two men's involvement in arranging equipment.

By the 1930s, realistic depictions of skilled laborers as portrayed in *Teeming Ingots* (fig. 9), however, were considered appropriate to celebrate contemporary working life. The strength, virility and intellect of the depicted men were understood as metaphors for their industries not necessarily as symbols of their own productivity. The industrial laborer as hero joined the revived agricultural ideal, the farmer, in the Depression era when the toll of unemployment made the "working-common man" a cult figure, focusing national attention for the first time, on an urban as well as a rural laborer.[24]

During these difficult economic times, artists who supported socialist ideals conveyed them in their representation of American technology and industry and in the choice of gender and ethnicity of workers. Many artists of the New Deal art programs idealized both the urban and rural laborer. Series of prints, a medium that was affordable to the average American, were similarly understood as a parallel to mural cycles that heroized the urban working class as in the lithographs *The People Work* (p. 52) or championed the rural worker as seen in the wood engravings *The Lumbercamp* (p. 51). Unfortunately, the depictions of workers in the ostensibly democratic art of a egalitarian nation—affordable and appealing original prints in both political and traditional subjects—failed to find buyers or to effect social change.

Women's Natural Work

In both Europe and America, twentieth-century artists perpetuated the academic tradition of idealizing subjects for the purpose of moral uplift or the contemplation of beauty. American artists, and by implication their patrons, intentionally or otherwise under-represented images of women in the workforce. Work associated with women's household duties or motherhood—essentially unpaid labor—was often interpreted as "non-work" in a picturesque mode that undercut the important status and contributions of women in society. Secular portrayals of motherhood, which often adapted religious iconography, were too easily recast in a sentimental guise that both diminished the profound associations of mother and child imagery and ignored the arduous demands of child rearing. Depictions of paid childcare followed similar conventions as in *The Luxembourg Garden, Paris* (fig. 10) where baby nurses play with their charges in a familial

24. Particularly helpful in the growing literature on the representation of the worker in the 1930s are Marlene Park and Gerald E. Markowitz, *Democratic Vistas: Post Offices and Public Art in the New Deal* (Philadelphia: Temple University Press, 1984) and Barbara Melosh, *Engendering Culture: Manhood and Womanhood in New Deal Public Art and Theater* (Washington, D.C.: Smithsonian Institution Press, 1991).

25. Linda Nochlin, "Morisot's *Wet Nurse*: The Construction of Work and Leisure in Impressionist Painting," in *Women Art and Power and Other Essays* (New York: Harper & Row, 1988): 37–56, and Elizabeth O'Leary, *At Beck and Call: The Representation of Domestic Servants in Nineteenth-Century American Painting* (Washington, D.C.: Smithsonian Institution Press, 1996).

22

9. JAMES EDWARD ALLEN

TEEMING INGOTS, 1935

10. MAURICE BRAZIL PRENDERGAST

THE LUXEMBOURG GARDEN, PARIS, 1892–94

26. Both authors document the political implications of women and weaving and sewing in American history. Laurel Thatcher Ulrich, *The Age of Homespun: Objects and Stories in the Creation of an American Myth* (New York: Knopf, 2001) and Marian Eastwood Wardle, *Genteel Production: Art and Labor in the Image of Women Sewing by Tarbell and Weir* (Ann Arbor: University Microfilms International, 1999).

27. Thorstein Veblen's *The Theory of the Leisure Class* (New York: Modern Library, 2001) is the standard reference for a critique of American materialism at the turn of the century.

28. For a discussion of the social ramifications of the French legalization of their sex industry on artistic production see T. J. Clark, "Olympia's Choice," in *The Painting of Modern Life: Paris in the Art of Manet and His Followers* (N.J.: Princeton University Press, 1984): 79–146.

29. Donna Gustafson, *Images From the World Between; The Circus in Twentieth Century American Art* (Cambridge, Mass.: MIT Press, 2001): 9–84.

manner. As quasi-family member and servant, the nursery maid labors within the confines of a social arrangement that denies any professional status and suggests that her labor is voluntary.[25]

For working-class women who cared for their children at home, labor often meant domestic tasks as well as piecework for the textile industry. The paid piecework produced by women in their homes was associated with their unpaid domestic duties thus suppressing the acknowledgement of their contribution to the labor force.[26] The introduction of sewing technology—the first machine was invented in 1851—into the home freed women from hours of hand sewing. Once sewing, whether by machine or hand, was removed from the worker's home it became another repetitive factory task in an industry setting, but at least was then considered a job rather than an extension of women's natural work.

The lack of a social agenda by most American artists is apparent by contrasting the idealized activity of the women peasants working by hand in *Breton Lacemakers* (p. 46) with the fragmented bodies of machine sewers in the *Sweat Shop* (p. 10). Equally notable is the conventional depiction of upper-class women at needlework, exemplified by *Unraveling Silk* (p. 47) where the genteel figure is part of the overall decorative pattern. A woman's unpaid production of non-utilitarian objects for conspicuous display—beautiful needlework—fulfilled the necessary requirements of elite women to be usefully occupied with a nonessential task thereby signifying her key role as the emblem of the leisure class.[27]

Within the fine arts, a remarkable case in masking women's work is the depiction of the sex industry, where women were portrayed in alluring settings and beautiful clothes. The intermingling of respectable women with ladies of the evening, a source of middle-class anxiety, was a scandalous yet intriguing attraction of the notorious Parisian nightlife speculated upon in *Café de nuit* (fig. 11). Despite legalized prostitution in France, public confusion arose over clandestine prostitution and the inability to differentiate between women who traded sexual relations for gifts and professionals who were self-employed in the sex trade.[28]

Artifice's Work

Society's ambivalence about women entertainers, whose charms were on public display and who seemed to enjoy the attention, as workers served to conceal their labor. In *Theater Scene* (p. 43), a blurred vision of the singers, the results of the dazzling flood lights, against the vibrant colors on the raised stage dominate the scene while the musicians at floor level are lost in the darkness with their backs to the audience. The relative anonymity of theatrical workers, aside from the notable exception of the "stars," contributed to their marginal status as workers.

The fascination with the circus as a subject for modern art began in late-nineteenth-century Paris with the "cult of the circus."[29] America's golden age of the circus continued into the 1920s when a version of P. T. Barnum's legendary "Greatest Show on Earth" was at its zenith as a popular leisure entertainment. Depictions of circus feats offered graceful protagonists in vividly colored costumes, or in some cases a risqué lack of dress, shown from an unusual perspectives

11. RICHARD EMIL (OR EDWARD) MILLER

CAFÉ DE NUIT, C. 1906

23

such as in *Elephant Act* (fig. 12) where the titillation of exposed flesh matched the daring deeds. Hours of training were required to develop their expertise, but entertainers subverted the notion of work as they presented themselves as a "natural" phenomenon. Artists reified the circus performers' illusion of play, seen in *Nouveau Cirque* (p. 42), with their spangled costumes and practiced smiles providing the ultimate dream, transforming work's drudgery into a seemingly joyful activity. Not all members of the circus community were skilled performers or talented entertainers. The "midway" was a sordid theatre of exotic dancers and "nature's accidents" gathered to stimulate an audience seeking the bizarre or unseemly. The circus's exhibition of bodies— grotesque or exquisitely formed, professional or amateur—was a spectacle of gyrating human motion, such as the bodies at work captured in *Pip and Flip* (p. 48).

Much like circus workers or popular entertainers, artists and their models labor to achieve an apparent spontaneity based on calculated artifice. Though the exchange between the artist and a model often appears naturalized, it is usually a system of labor for payment. Artists' models are often romantically perceived as more muse than employee but the slumped posture in *Nude Girl, Miss Leslie Hall* (p. 49) conveys the reality of physical fatigue—an outcome of holding a pose over an extended time. Paid to physically disrobe, the model, nonetheless, guards her psychological vulnerability by veiling her thoughts behind her withdrawn expression. The fine line that separates the artist's model from that of the exotic dancer or stripper, portrayed in *Striptease at New Gotham* (p. 10),

is one of numbers and movement. While the model's work requires her to be a vehicle through which the artistic creativity of an individual is channeled, the dancer's job calls for a performance that demands creativity and interaction with an audience.[30]

An artist depicting another artist at work is an artistic paradox. Is this a mirrored reflection of a skilled professional or a moment of inspired genius? James McNeill Whistler meticulously labored over his drypoint of *Riault, the Engraver* (fig. 13) simultaneously as the older man bent over his own plate with tool in hand. Whistler's famous response to the query of why he charged a large fee for a painting that required only two days work neatly sums up this artistic challenge: "I ask it for the knowledge I have gained in the work of a life time."[31] While all art is an illusion, perhaps, the greatest artifice of all is the invisibility of artistic labor, even more ironic portraying entertainers at work.

As America matured as a nation, political rhetoric continued to emphasize the democratic ideal of the common man as represented by the rural worker—a metaphor for hard work, moral turpitude, and self-reliance. The cult of the farmer was ultimately overturned in the midst of the 1890s

30. Frances Pohl, "The Miner and the Burlesque Dancer: Work and Gender in the 1930s," in *In the Eye of the Storm: An Art of the Conscience, 1930–70, Selections from the Collection of Philip J. and Suzanne Schiller* (San Francisco: Pomegranate Art Books, 1995): 15–36.

31. Quoted in Linda Merrill, *A Pot of Paint: Aesthetics on Trail in Whistler v. Ruskin* (Washington, D.C.: Smithsonian Institution Press, 1992): 145–48.

32. See footnote 5.

13. JAMES ABBOTT MCNEILL WHISTLER

RIAULT, THE ENGRAVER, 1860

24

12. ROBERT RIGGS

ELEPHANT ACT, C. 1935

as industrial titans and middle-class art patrons sought non-threatening images of happy workers. Paradoxically, the deluge of European immigrants to the United States seeking dignified employment prompted an art world phenomenon in which the elite clamored for images of the archaic European peasant. Reinforcing these images of rural workers as content in the hierarchy of workers were countless representations of entertainers and others, whose happy countenances masked their exertions while serving those at leisure. At the same time, subtle but disturbing reflections of the class stratification of women's labor were easily overlooked as they were cloaked in dutiful assumptions about the roles of housewives or mothers. The renowned Puritan work ethic associated with America was never overtly celebrated in fine arts as much as it was implied indirectly. Most painters suppressed labor's harsh reality in their art, abdicating the role of social commentary to artists employed in the graphic arts and later photojournalism.

During the international economic turmoil of the 1930s, the visual discourse of labor as an emblem of national identity was translated into new responses. For the first time, images of the urban worker vied with the agricultural worker as symbols of the American common man. Economic recovery in the following decade and the trauma of a world war encouraged the American public to experience a nostalgic longing for a mythic past where mankind lived in harmony with nature. Throughout the twentieth century, the cowboy, lionized more in American popular culture than in art, became the new pastoral hero. Significantly, the cowboy also was identified internationally as representing American values associated with democracy and laissez-faire capitalism.

Majestically astride their horses in an unsullied Western landscape, the cowboys portrayed in *The Cow Country* (fig. 14) returned to de Crèvecœur's vision of a citizen-farmer as "unfettered and unrestrained, because each person works for himself."[32] As a protagonist who sings as he wrangles cattle on the open range, the American cowboy, ironically, reflects Virgil's pastoral ideal of the shepherd of Arcadia rather than the industrious farmer. American artists' contribution to the mythology of the worker, however, was innovative and potent when linked to expressions of national identity embodied in images of the farmer and the cowboy—uniquely American perspectives on work.

14. MAYNARD DIXON
THE COW COUNTRY, 1938

James Edward Allen (1894–1964)
Teeming Ingots, 1935
Etching, 11 7/8 x 9 15/16 in. (30.2 x 25.2 cm)
TFA 1995.23

Henry Bacon (1839–1912)
Lady in Boat, 1879
Oil on canvas, 19 5/8 x 28 5/8 in. (48.9 x 72.7 cm)
TFA 1996.88

Gifford Beal (1879–1956)
Pulling in the Nets #1, c. 1930
Etching and drypoint, 7 1/4 x 14 1/4 in.
(18.4 x 36.2 cm)
TFA 1996.77
The Swordfisherman, c. 1930
Etching and drypoint on ivory laid paper,
9 1/16 x 11 7/8 in. (23 x 30.2 cm)
TFA 1996.76

George Wesley Bellows (1882–1925)
Nude Girl, Miss Leslie Hall, 1909
Oil on canvas, 60 x 42 in. (152.4 x 106.7 cm)
TFA 1999.5

Thomas Hart Benton (1885–1975)
Huck Finn, 1936
Lithograph on wove Rives paper,
16 9/16 x 21 5/8 in. (42.1 x 54.9 cm)
TFA 1995.24

George Caleb Bingham (1811–1879)
The Jolly Flatboatmen, 1877–78
Oil on canvas, 26 1/16 x 36 3/8 in. (66.2 x 92.4 cm)
TFA 1992.15

Frank Myers Boggs (1855–1926)
Street Scene in Paris, 1878
Oil on canvas, 37 1/2 x 59 in. (95.3 x 149.9 cm)
TFA 1999.12

Alfred Thompson Bricher (1837–1908)
*The Sidewheeler "The City of St. Paul"
on the Mississippi River, Dubuque, Iowa*, 1872
Oil on canvas mounted on board,
20 1/8 x 38 1/8 in. (51.1 x 96.8 cm)
TFA 1992.18

George de Forest Brush (1855–1941)
The Weaver, 1889
Oil on canvas, 12 x 15 in. (30.5 x 38.1 cm)
TFA 1988.23

Dennis Miller Bunker (1861–1890)
Brittany Town Morning, Larmor, 1884
Oil on canvas, 14 x 22 in. (35.6 x 55.9 cm)
TFA 1991.1

Jefferson David Chalfant (1856–1931)
The Blacksmith, 1907
Oil on canvas, 25 3/4 x 33 1/2 in. (65.4 x 85.1 cm)
TFA 1999.3

Samuel Colman, Jr. (1832–1920)
Ships Unloading, New York, 1868
Oil on canvas mounted on board,
42 x 30 1/4 in. (106.7 x 76.8 cm)
TFA 1984.4

Eanger Irving Couse (1866–1936)
Making Pottery, 1912
Oil on canvas, 35 1/4 x 46 1/4 in. (89.5 x 117.5 cm)
TFA 1999.33

Louis Paul Dessar (1867–1952)
Peasant Woman and Haystacks, Giverny, 1892
Oil on canvas, 18 1/4 x 13 in. (46.4 x 33 cm)
TFA 1993.9

Maynard Dixon (1875–1946)
✻ *The Cow Country*, 1938
Oil on canvas, 30 x 40 in. (76.2 x 101.6 cm)
The Eiteljorg Museum of American Indians
and Western Art,
1989.2.60

August Franzen (1863–1938)
Late Afternoon Sun, 1890
Watercolor and gouache on cream wove paper,
26 7/16 x 38 3/16 in. (67.2 x 97 cm)
TFA 1987.19

Frederick Carl Frieseke (1874–1939)
Unraveling Silk, c. 1915
Oil on canvas, 32 1/4 x 32 3/8 in. (81.9 x 82.2 cm)
TFA 1992.35

CHECKLIST
TO THE EXHIBITION

Sanford Robinson Gifford (1823–1880)
Hunter Mountain, Twilight, 1866
Oil on canvas, 30 5/8 x 54 1/8 in. (77.8 x 137.5 cm)
TFA 1999.57

Boris Gorelick (1911–1984)
Sweat Shop, c. 1936–39
Lithograph on ivory wove paper,
11 7/8 x 15 7/16 in. (30.2 x 39.3 cm)
TFA 1996.70

William Groombridge (1748–1811)
*View of a Manor House on the Harlem River,
New York,* 1793
Oil on canvas, 39 3/4 x 49 in. (101 x 124.5 cm)
TFA 1992.37

Bernhard Gutmann (1863–1936)
Breton Lacemakers, 1912
Oil on canvas, 32 x 39 1/2 in. (81.3 x 100.3 cm)
TFA 1988.18

Frederick Childe Hassam (1859–1935)
French Peasant Girl, c. 1883
Oil on canvas, 21 5/8 x 13 7/8 in. (54.9 x 35.2 cm)
TFA 1989.21
Une Averse, rue Bonaparte, 1887
Oil on canvas, 40 3/8 x 77 7/16 in.
(102.6 x 196.7 cm)
TFA 1993.20
Horse Drawn Cabs at Evening, New York, c. 1890
Watercolor, 14 x 17 3/4 in. (35.6 x 45.1 cm)
TFA 1999.66

Winslow Homer (1836–1910)
The Gleaners, 1867
Oil on panel, 6 x 18 in. (15.2 x 45.7 cm)
TFA 1999.76
Haymakers, 1867
Oil on canvas, 13 1/8 x 18 1/4 in. (33.3 x 46.4 cm)
TFA 1989.9
The Nurse, 1867
Oil on panel, 19 x 11 in. (48.3 x 27.9 cm)
TFA 1999.74
The Life Line, 1884
Etching printed in blue, on cream wove paper,
12 7/8 x 17 3/4 in. (32.7 x 45.1 cm)
TFA 1996.8

John Frederick Kensett (1816–1872)
Almy Pond, Newport, 1855–59
Oil on canvas, 12 5/8 x 22 1/8 in. (32.1 x 56.2 cm)
TFA 1992.42

Rockwell Kent (1882–1971)
Cranberrying, Monhegan, c. 1907
Oil on canvas, 28 1/16 x 38 1/4 in. (71.3 x 97.2 cm)
TFA C1983.4

John Lewis Krimmel (1786–1821)
Blind Fiddler, 1812
Oil on canvas, 16 5/8 x 22 1/16 in. (42.2 x 56 cm)
TFA 1999.81

Walt Kuhn (1877–1942)
Clown with Drum, 1942
Oil on canvas, 60 7/8 x 41 3/8 in. (154.6 x 105.1 cm)
TFA 1992.172

Fitz Hugh Lane (1804–1865)
Gloucester Harbor, 1856
Oil on canvas, 22 3/8 x 36 1/16 in. (56.8 x 91.6 cm)
TFA 1993.21

Clare Leighton (1901–1989)
The Lumbercamp – Limbing, 1931
Wood engraving, 8 1/2 x 12 in. (21.6 x 30.5 cm)
TFA 1996.33.b
The Lumbercamp – Loading, 1931
Wood engraving, 8 15/16 x 11 7/8 in. (22.7 x 30.2 cm)
TFA 1996.33.c
The Lumbercamp – Landing, 1931
Wood engraving, 8 15/16 x 12 1/2 in. (22.7 x 31.8 cm)
TFA 1996.33.d
The Lumbercamp – Resting, 1931
Wood engraving, 9 1/16 x 11 1/16 in. (23 x 28.1 cm)
TFA 1996.33.e
The Lumbercamp – Breaking Camp, 1931
Wood engraving, 11 7/16 x 8 in. (29.1 x 20.3 cm)
TFA 1996.33.f

William Henry Lippincott (1849–1920)
The Cliffs at Étretat, 1890
Oil on canvas, 10 3/4 x 14 1/16 in. (27.3 x 35.7 cm)
TFA 1992.173

George Benjamin Luks (1867–1933)
Knitting for the Soldiers: High Bridge Park, c. 1918
Oil on canvas, 30 3/16 x 36 1/8 in. (76.7 x 91.8 cm)
TFA 1999.87

Mary Fairchild MacMonnies (later Low)
(1858–1946)
Dans la nursery, 1897–98
Oil on canvas, 32 x 17 in. (81.3 x 43.2 cm)
TFA 1999.91

Reginald Marsh (1898–1954)
Pip and Flip, 1932
Tempera on paper mounted on canvas,
48 1/4 x 48 1/4 in. (122.6 x 122.6 cm)
TFA 1999.96
Striptease at New Gotham, 1935
Etching, 11 15/16 x 8 15/16 in. (30.3 x 22.7 cm)
TFA 1995.17
The Barker, 1931
Etching on cream laid paper,
9 7/8 x 7 7/8 in. (25.1 x 20 cm)
TFA 1995.44

Richard Emil (or Edward) Miller (1875–1943)
Café de nuit, c. 1906
Oil on canvas, 48 1/2 x 67 3/8 in. (123.2 x 171.1 cm)
TFA 1999.97

Charles Moeller (1855–1930)
The Chemist, c. 1875
Oil on canvas, 8 x 12 in. (20.3 x 30.5 cm)
TFA 1999.98

William Sidney Mount (1807–1868)
The Trap Sprung, 1844
Oil on panel, 12 7/8 x 17 1/16 in. (32.7 x 43.3 cm)
TFA 1992.52

Charles Sprague Pearce (1851–1914)
Evening (Auvers-sur-Oise), c. 1885
Oil on canvas, 41 x 69 1/4 in. (104.1 x 175.9 cm)
TFA 1994.15

Maurice Brazil Prendergast (1858–1924)
Bareback Rider, 1894–95
Monotype on cream wove paper, laid down
on cream wove paper,
11 3/4 x 7 1/2 in. (29.8 x 19.1 cm)
TFA 1992.70
Nouveau Cirque, 1894–95
Monotype on greyish-ivory China paper,
laid down, 15 1/4 x 14 1/2 in. (38.7 x 36.8 cm)
TFA 1992.95
The Luxembourg Garden, Paris, 1892–94
Oil on canvas, 12 7/8 x 9 5/8 in. (32.7 x 24.4 cm)
TFA 1992.68

Frederic Remington (1861–1909)
* *Trailing Texas Cattle*, c. 1904
Oil on canvas, 30 1/2 x 51 1/2 in. (77.5 x 130.9 cm)
The Buffalo Bill Historical Center,
Loan from Private Collection,
L.21.92.1

Robert Riggs (1896–1970)
Elephant Act, c. 1935
Lithograph on cream wove paper,
14 5/16 x 19 9/16 in. (36.4 x 49.7 cm)
TFA 1996.42
Tumblers, 1934
Lithograph on cream wove paper, 14 1/4 x 19 in.
(36.2 x 48.3 cm)
TFA 1996.43

Charles M. Russell (1865–1926)
* *Bronc in Cow Camp*, 1897
Oil on canvas, 20 1/8 x 31 1/4 in. (51.1 x 79.4 cm)
Amon Carter Museum, Fort Worth, Texas,
1964.144
(exhibited only at the Terra Museum
of American Art in Chicago)

John Singer Sargent (1856–1925)
Breton Woman with a Basket, sketch for *The Oyster Gatherers of Cancale*, 1877
Oil on canvas, 18 ½ x 11 ¾ in. (47 x 29.8 cm)
TFA 1996.53
Young Boy on the Beach, sketch for *The Oyster Gatherers of Cancale*, 1877
Oil on canvas, 17 ¼ x 10 ¼ in. (43.8 x 26 cm)
TFA 1999.132
A Parisian Beggar Girl, c. 1880
Oil on canvas, 25 3/8 x 17 3/16 in. (64.5 x 43.7 cm)
TFA 1994.14
Dennis Miller Bunker Painting at Calcot, 1888
Oil on canvas mounted on masonite,
27 x 25 ¼ in. (68.6 x 64.1 cm)
TFA 1999.130

Everett Shinn (1876–1953)
Theater Scene, 1903
Oil on canvas, 12 ¾ x 15 ½ in. (32.4 x 39.4 cm)
TFA 1999.136

Raphael Soyer (1889–1987)
The Mission, 1933
Lithograph on cream wove paper,
12 1/8 x 17 5/8 in. (30.4 x 44.8 cm)
TFA 1996.66

Robert Spencer (1879–1931)
Washerwomen, n.d.
Oil on canvas, 14 x 12 1/8 in. (35.6 x 30.8 cm)
TFA C1991.3

Benton Spruance (1904–1967)
The People Work – Morning, 1937
Lithograph, 13 11/16 x 18 15/16 in. (34.8 x 48.1 cm)
TFA 1995.47.a
The People Work – Noon, 1937
Lithograph, 13 13/16 x 18 15/16 in. (35.1 x 48.1 cm)
TFA 1995.47.b
The People Work – Evening, 1937
Lithograph, 13 13/16 x 18 15/16 in. (35.1 x 48.1 cm)
TFA 1995.47.c
The People Work – Night, 1937
Lithograph, 13 11/16 x 18 15/16 in. (34.8 x 48.1 cm)
TFA 1995.47.d

Charles Frederick Ulrich (1858–1908)
The Village Printing Shop, Haarlem, Holland, 1884
Oil on panel, 21 ¼ x 22 15/16 in. (54 x 58.3 cm)
TFA 1992.137

Robert Vonnoh (1858–1933)
La Sieste (The Rest), 1887
Oil on panel, 8 ½ x 10 9/16 in. (21.6 x 26.8 cm)
TFA 1992.139

James Abbott McNeill Whistler (1834–1903)
Beggars, after 1880
Drypoint etching on cream Japanese paper,
11 15/16 x 8 5/16 in. (30.3 x 21.1 cm)
TFA 1994.8
The Lime-Burner, 1859
Etching and drypoint on thin cream
Japanese paper, 9 7/8 x 7 in. (25.1 x 17.8 cm)
TFA 1995.4
Riault, the Engraver, 1860
Drypoint on cream laid paper, 8 7/8 x 5 7/8 in.
(22.5 x 14.9 cm)
TFA 1995.53

Thomas Waterman Wood (1823–1903)
The Yankee Pedlar, 1872
Oil on canvas, 28 x 40 in. (71.1 x 101.6 cm)
TFA 1998.3

Robert Wylie (1839–1877)
Les Modèles de Pont-Aven, c. 1875
Oil on canvas, 21 ½ x 29 ¼ in. (54.6 x 74.3 cm)
TFA 1992.166

WILLIAM GROOMBRIDGE

VIEW OF A MANOR HOUSE ON THE HARLEM RIVER,
NEW YORK, 1793

JOHN LEWIS KRIMMEL

BLIND FIDDLER, 1812

WINSLOW HOMER

THE GLEANERS, 1867

FITZ HUGH LANE

GLOUCESTER HARBOR, 1856

SAMUEL COLMAN, JR.

SHIPS UNLOADING, NEW YORK, 1868

WINSLOW HOMER

THE NURSE, 1867

ROBERT SPENCER

WASHERWOMEN, N.D.

38

CHARLES MOELLER

THE CHEMIST, C. 1875

39

CHARLES FREDERICK ULRICH

THE VILLAGE PRINTING SHOP,

HAARLEM, HOLLAND, 1884

FREDERICK CHILDE HASSAM

FRENCH PEASANT GIRL, C. 1883

40

AUGUST FRANZEN

LATE AFTERNOON SUN, 1890

42

MAURICE BRAZIL PRENDERGAST

NOUVEAU CIRQUE, 1894–95

EVERETT SHINN

THEATER SCENE, 1903

JEFFERSON DAVID CHALFANT

THE BLACKSMITH, 1907

EANGER IRVING COUSE

MAKING POTTERY, 1912

BERNHARD GUTMANN

BRETON LACEMAKERS, 1912

FREDERICK CARL FRIESEKE

UNRAVELING SILK, C. 1915

REGINALD MARSH

PIP AND FLIP, 1932

GEORGE WESLEY BELLOWS

NUDE GIRL, MISS LESLIE HALL, 1909

GIFFORD BEAL

THE SWORDFISHERMAN, C. 1930

CLARE LEIGHTON

THE LUMBERCAMP — LANDING, 1931

BENTON SPRUANCE

THE PEOPLE WORK — MORNING, 1937

THE PEOPLE WORK — NOON, 1937

THE PEOPLE WORK — EVENING, 1937

THE PEOPLE WORK — NIGHT, 1937

SELECTED
BIBLIOGRAPHY

Adams, Steven. *The Barbizon School and the Origins of Impressionism.* London: Phaidon Press, 1994.

Bermingham, Peter. *American Art in the Barbizon Mood.* Washington, D.C.: Smithsonian Institution Press, 1975.

Brettell, Richard R. and Caroline B. Brettell. *Painters and Peasants in the Nineteenth Century.* New York: Rizzoli, 1983.

Burns, Sarah. *Pastoral Inventions: Rural Life in Nineteenth-Century American Art and Culture.* Philadelphia: Temple University Press, 1989.

Clark, T. J. *The Painting of Modern Life: Paris in the Art of Manet and His Followers.* Princeton: Princeton University Press, 1984.

Dabakis, Melissa. "The Individual vs. the Collective: Images of the American Worker in the 1920s." *The Journal of the Society for Industrial Archeology* 12, no. 2 (1986): 51–62.

Fishwick, Marshall W. "The Cowboy: America's Contribution to the World's Mythology." *Western Folklore* 11 (1951–52): 77–92.

Goetzmann, William H. and William N. Goetzmann. *The West of the Imagination.* New York: W. W. Norton Company, 1986.

Gustafson, Donna. *Images From the World Between; The Circus in Twentieth-Century American Art.* Cambridge: MIT Press, 2001.

Herbert, Robert. "City vs. Country: The Rural Images in French Paintings from Millet to Gauguin." *Artforum* 8 (February 1970): 44–55.

Jacobs, Michael. *The Good and Simple Life:
Artists Colonies in Europe and America*. Oxford:
Phaidon, 1985.

Johns, Elizabeth. *American Genre Painting:
The Politics of Everyday Life*.
New Haven: Yale University Press, 1991.

Kennedy, Elizabeth. "Charlie Russell's
Log Studio: The Origin of the Museum
of Western Art." *Journal of the West* 40, no. 4
(Fall 2001): 60–66.

Lears, T. J. Jackson. *No Place of Grace:
Antimodernism and the Transformation
of American Culture, 1880–1920*.
Chicago: University of Chicago Press, 1981.

Lübbren, Nina. *Rural Artists' Colonies in Europe
1870–1910*. New Brunswick, N.J.: Rutgers
University Press, 2001, 40–63.

Melosh, Barbara. *Engendering Culture: Manhood
and Womanhood in New Deal Public Art and Theater*.
Washington, D.C.: Smithsonian Institution
Press, 1991.

Nochlin, Linda. "Morisot's *Wet Nurse*:
The Construction of Work and Leisure
in Impressionist Painting." In *Women Art and Power
and Other Essays*. New York: Harper & Row, 1988.

O'Leary, Elizabeth. *At Beck and Call:
The Representation of Domestic Servants
in Nineteenth-Century American Painting*.
Washington, D.C.: Smithsonian Institution
Press, 1996.

Park, Marlene and Gerald E. Markowitz.
*Democratic Vistas: Post Offices and Public Art
in the New Deal*. Philadelphia: Temple University
Press, 1984.

Pohl, Frances. *In the Eye of the Storm:
An Art of the Conscience, 1930–1970, Selections
from the Collection of Philip J. and Suzanne Schiller*.
San Francisco: Pomegranate Art Books, 1995.

Pyne, Kathleen A. *Art and the Higher Life:
Painting and Evolutionary Thought
in Late-Nineteenth-Century America*. Austin:
University of Texas Press, 1996.

Savage, Jr. William W. *The Cowboy Hero:
His Image in American History and Culture*.
Norman: University of Oklahoma Press, 1979.

Spencer, Harold. "J. Alden Weir and the Image
of the American Farm." In *A Connecticut Place:
Weir Farm An American Painter's Rural Retreat*.
Wilton, Conn.: Weir Farm Trust and The National
Park Service, 2000, 42–75.

Slotkin, Richard. *Gunfighter Nation: The Myth
of the Frontier in Twentieth-Century America*.
New York: Harper Perennial, 1993.

Ulrich, Laurel Thatcher. *The Age of Homespun:
Objects and Stories in the Creation
of an American Myth*. New York: Knopf, 2001.